PERSPECTIVE!

SHIFTING INTO THE
REALITY OF LOVE

NANCY WHITTON

BALBOA.
PRESS

A DIVISION OF HAY HOUSE

Balboa Press books may be ordered through booksellers or by contacting:

Balboa Press
A Division of Hay House
1663 Liberty Drive
Bloomington, IN 47403
www.balboapress.com
1 (877) 407-4847

Because of the dynamic nature of the Internet, any web addresses or
links contained in this book may have changed since publication and
may no longer be valid. The views expressed in this work are solely those
of the author and do not necessarily reflect the views of the publisher,
and the publisher hereby disclaims any responsibility for them.

The author of this book does not dispense medical advice or prescribe
the use of any technique as a form of treatment for physical, emotional,
or medical problems without the advice of a physician, either directly
or indirectly. The intent of the author is only to offer information
of a general nature to help you in your quest for emotional and
spiritual well-being. In the event you use any of the information in
this book for yourself, which is your constitutional right, the author
and the publisher assume no responsibility for your actions.

Any people depicted in stock imagery provided by Thinkstock are
models, and such images are being used for illustrative purposes only.
Certain stock imagery © Thinkstock.

Printed in the United States of America.

ISBN: 978-1-4525-8989-3 (sc)
ISBN: 978-1-4525-8990-9 (e)

Library of Congress Control Number: 2014900250

Balboa Press rev. date: 02/13/2014

I dedicate this book
to George my beloved husband
to my mom and dad and sisters
to Elizabeth, Josh, Grace and Rue
and to You

Many thanks to my dear friends and mentors Martha Creek and Lin Schussler Williams. I am grateful for wisdom expressed and shared by Jerry Boyland, Larry Watson, Alan Cohen, Patrick Cameron, Peace Pilgrim, Emmet Fox and Susan Douthitt. Unending love and appreciation to my friends and teachers Revs. Pat and Jack Barker.

A Note to Readers: Using QR Codes to Access the Music in this Book

A QR Code is a bar code that can be scanned by a Smart Phone camera.

In order to scan a QR Code you will need:
-a Smart Phone with a camera
-an app that reads QR Codes which include:
        -NeoReader (iPhone)
        -ScanLife (Blackberry)
        -Quick Mark (Android)
-a crisp QR Code like the ones in this book

Alternately, you may simply go to this link to find the songs in sequence: www.nancywhitton.com

---

*The most important decision we make is whether we believe
we live in a friendly or hostile universe. Albert Einstein*

*From that decision we decide how we will respond
to the world and how we will interpret the events
that come into our lives. Ray Davis*

When we choose one point of view, we let go of the other.

Let's Begin

I feel deep sadness; hardly any joy or happiness.
I feel like a waterfall is suspended, frozen in time,
behind my face, waiting for me to say yes to it's flow.
I feel disconnected from God, me and others – all others!

This was my journal entry a few days before I noticed a corner of blackness in my left eye. "If it doesn't clear by the weekend, I'll call the ophthalmologist," was my thought. When the darkness neared my central vision, I got on the phone. The emergency visit to the eye doctor's office confirmed I had a detached retina.

This seemed like the physical manifestation of the detachment I was feeling in my life. I was disconnected from myself and my loved ones. I was disconnected from enthusiasm, passion, peace, joy and purpose.

On Monday my eye was repaired.

As I was pulled by some invisible force through the days and weeks of my healing, fear arose in mighty splendor. Yes, I was afraid about what might happen to my eyesight. But other fears from my past and about the future, both big and small, propelled themselves into the present moment. It was as if they were all clamoring to be dealt with compassionately and openly. I made the decision to do just that.

To my relief and delight I found that the light of wisdom and love were always present to help me see my way through the darkness. The light was there to guide me through my next step which generally took me to greater peace.

These are stories of personal transformation. I wrote them to remind myself of wisdom revealed, lessons learned. I wrote them to remember how to move through my fears and return to love and a sense of wholeness and joy.

It's important to know that we can discover helpful insights and manageable, amazing solutions to our challenges. We can discover and use beautiful practices to comfort and support ourselves through our pain and to enliven us to our natural joy and the wonder of life and living.

Gratefully and with true humility I open my heart and extend my hand to you. Let's walk this healing path and take the journey into wholeness together.

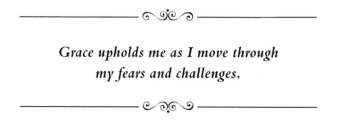

Grace upholds me as I move through my fears and challenges.

Longing

I went out to garden this hot summer evening. Well, it's not officially summer but the 90 plus degree weather makes it seem like mid July in the mid west. It's the kind of weather where I am moist all over even before I get my garden gloves on. I feel healthy and energized. My garden is looking healthy and energized this season – the plants stand so tall and lush. It's almost as if they are bragging about their beauty. I just smile.

I haven't wanted to do much in the way of gardening the last several years. This season is different. With every weed I pull, with every seed or seedling I plant, I feel as if I am coming alive again. It's a good feeling and I am curious about what this could mean.

While digging, I notice a storm brewing in the distance. The sky is dark to the north. My skin senses the temperature dropping degree by degree and I find myself beckoning to the clouds, "Come this way, come over here and water my little piece of heaven!" When the wind becomes fierce and the sky quite black, I reluctantly head for my house with a squeal of delight. The probability of rain is increasing with every hurried step.

Thunder, lightning and rain saturate the earth and my soul feels strangely refreshed. Sometimes, I wonder if I should just step out of the chaos of life and plant melons and tomatoes. There is an orderly pattern emerging here and I experience such comfort and safety within the confines of this little plot. All the while my heart is silently singing: There Is Only Love.

I wonder if the world would miss my song if I stayed solidly rooted in the fenced in area behind my house. I wonder if my heart could stand the isolation even in the midst of such exquisite beauty. I entreat nature to share her wisdom with me; to allow answers to reveal themselves as systematically and effortlessly as the moon appears to rise. I want to know.

Song by David Kisor: Bend Willow Bend

Bend Willow Bend by David Kisor

Bend, willow bend
Till your branches touch the ground
Fly, snowbird fly
Till a warmer home is found

Turn, seasons turn, burn, wildfire burn
Take me with you as you go
There's so much I don't know
There's a lot I want to learn

Dance, thistle dance
In the rustling of the breeze
Flow, river flow
Till your waters kiss the seas

Die, sunset die, rise, half moon rise
Take me with you as you go
There's so much I don't know
There's a lot I want to try

From the earth to the stars, all the dreams you are
As you rise to fall, teach me all

So when I die I'm not afraid of death
Having lived my life till there's no living left
Like my weeping friend
Grow to touch my roots again

So bend, willow bend

From the earth to the stars, all the dreams you are
As you rise to fall, teach me all

So when I die I'm not afraid of death
Having lived my life till there's no living left
Like my weeping friend
Grow to touch my roots again

So bend, willow bend

Thought

Thoughts arise out of our life experiences. We form ideas about what this all means to us, about us, about others and life. We assume we are correct in conjuring up what these experiences are saying. We assume what others say about us and about life is correct. We usually never question our creations/our beliefs, but we live by them religiously.

Thought is creative.
Our thoughts and beliefs can be fearful and limiting, or they can be expansive, positive and full of possibility. But whatever we choose to think, that is the way it is for us.

In the past, I have attached my happiness and sadness to what happens in the world. Backwards! My happiness and sadness are generated by my interpretation of what happens, not by the actual event that takes place.

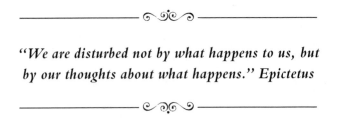

"We are disturbed not by what happens to us, but by our thoughts about what happens." Epictetus

When we really get that our experience of life is a reflection of our thinking, then we become mindful of choosing thoughts that mirror back to us the peace and happiness we desire. Whatever we send out returns to us. Naturally, we want to give what we would be glad and grateful to receive.

All of my thoughts are in support
of my best life ever!
Patrick Cameron

Song by Karen Drucker and Joyce Ripp: I Send My Love

I Send My Love

Music: Karen Drucker; Words: Joyce Ripp
from Songs of the Spirit
Copyright: TayToones Music, BMI

I send my love over the mountains
I send my love over the sea
I send my love into the heavens
And it returns to me…

I send my love over the mountains
I send my love over the sea
I send my love into the heavens
And it returns to me…

I send my joy over the mountains
I send my joy over the sea
I send my joy into the heavens
And it returns to me…

I send my power over the mountains
I send my power over the sea
I send my power into the heavens
And it returns to me…

I send peace over the mountains
I send peace over the sea
I send peace into the heavens
And it returns to me…

I send my power over the mountains
I send my power over the sea
I send my power into the heavens
And it returns to me…

I send my love over the mountains
I send my love over the sea
I send my love into the heavens
And it returns to me…
And it returns to me…
And it returns to me…

It returns to me…
It returns to me…
It returns to me…

A Case of Mistaken Identity

When I was a little girl, I spent the night with my cousins. This was a real treat for me and my sister. I have no recollection of most of that experience, but I do remember having cereal for breakfast the next morning. After I ate all of my cornflakes, there was a pretty big bowl of milk left. My aunt asked me why I hadn't told her I didn't want that much milk. "Look what you've wasted," she snapped. I sat silently interpreting what happened to mean that I was wasteful! I placed that thought in a little corner of my mind and though that incident was long forgotten, unconsciously, I played that self judgment out in present time through the years.

That was wasteful! I was wasteful! That was the thought I created from that experience. And, I believed it! When we identify with a thought (believe it) we're saying to ourselves, that's who I am – the girl who is wasteful. Then our minds go to work finding proof that this is so.

My point in sharing this story is that we don't have to let the past define who we are and how we will act in this present moment. We don't have to let a situation or anyone define who we are. Who we are, has already been determined. We are made in the image and likeness of goodness and we can align our thoughts about ourselves with the goodness that we are at our core

If a thought doesn't align with the truth of who I am, I can change it. It could be helpful to change that thought! It could be fun to change that thought! Let's have some fun!

My dear friend and fabulous Coach Lin Schussler Williams shared this 9 word, life changing process with me. It can help us lay down the dead weight of limited, fearful thinking.

Up until now…
I am willing…
No matter what.

We begin by stating our old belief/behavior/fear, with the words; up until now. Then we shift perspective/open to a new possibility beginning with the words: I am willing (to see it/do it differently) and then we seal the deal with the words: no matter what.

Up until now, I thought I was wasteful if I did something for myself that I really wanted but went above and beyond my needs. Now I am willing to see how valuable it is to listen and respond to the promptings of my heart. I allow **joy and wisdom** to inform my choices – no matter what.

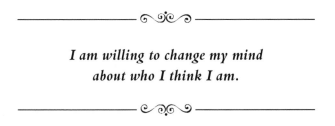

*I am willing to change my mind
about who I think I am.*

Who We Are

We are spiritual beings having a human experience. I've heard that statement many, many times. It is a convenient way to talk about who we are.

Our human nature is of the world. We have bodies, brains, thoughts and feelings – all part of and comfortable in the material world of form. All form will some day dissolve and so it is sometimes referred to as an illusion. We access the world of form through our senses. We judge by appearances. Our ego selves are part of our human personality. Fear, separation, lack and limitation are hallmarks of the ego.

Our spiritual nature is formless and consists of the pure energy of being. We sometimes refer to this pure energy as God, goodness, Spirit, Creator, Source and even Life. This energy is whole and complete and nothing or no one can ever change that. In Spirit, we cannot be hurt or damaged in any way. As spiritual beings, we are connected to God our Source and therefore, to all creation.

Because the pure energy of being is eternal, it is real. It is the real of who we are. This is our essential nature. We are the essence of divine peace and unconditional love. When we express Spirit/the spirit of love through our humanity, we are expressing our authentic selves. This is our natural state of being. I know that this is where I want to live my life from…the consciousness of love.

I allow my human self to be a
vehicle for expressing
the pure energy of life.

I am love expressing!

I am the radiant joy of being.

Song by Jody and Gary Soland: Inside of Me

Inside of Me by Jody and Gary Soland

Inside of me, I see heaven
Inside of me, the promised land
A place of joy, of love and peace
Inside of me, inside of me

Inside of me, a spiritual treasure
Inside of me more precious than gold
Everything I want and everything I need
Is inside of me, inside of me

And I could search the whole world
For the treasure I seek
Or I can look
Inside of me

Inside of me, is a beautiful light
Inside of me, all the wisdom I need
To teach me everyday, and guide me on my way
Inside of me, inside of me

And I could search the whole world
For the answers I seek
Or I can look
Inside of me

Inside of me, there is only love
Inside of me, I know the truth
That who I really am, is the child of God I seek
Inside of me, inside of me

And I could search the whole world
For the truth that I seek
Or I could look
Inside of me

Oh, I could search the whole world
For the love that I seek
Or I could look
Inside of me,
Inside of me.

Fear

Fears are scary beliefs we set up for ourselves with the intent of keeping our human selves safe. Fear lives in future time and so it often seems like a figment of my imagination. Fear also can seem very real. My fears used to scare the heck out of me! When I noticed them, I would run fast and far in the opposite direction.

Over time, I've come to see that fears are part of the human experience. Maybe the purpose of fear is to support us in developing confidence in ourselves and trust in the Universe. Maybe fear is pointing us in the direction of our wisdom and strength. Fear longs to keep us in our comfort zone and our souls are always inviting us to step into new territory. It used to feel so stressful wanting to soar and feeling afraid to, at the same time. I now consider this back and forth motion, the natural, playful tug of war between our egos and our evolving souls.

Sometimes, I actually find myself being grateful for my fears. They are like dear friends calling me home to my heart. They ask and sometimes insist that I be present to them to hear what they are trying to tell me. Running away from my fears only seems to make them more persistent or it drives them more deeply into my unconscious mind where they direct the parts I'm allowed to play in life.

Maybe…maybe we can just be aware of our fearful thoughts and not believe them. We can listen to what they have to tell us about what we must be believing about ourselves. When we know those thoughts, we can explore them, change them…if we like.

One evening I felt such sweet compassion for my whole self – including my fears. I didn't want to disown them or shut them out. I didn't want to run and hide or be angry with myself for feeling fearful – again. I just wanted to do something that felt kind and comforting. I wanted to sing a love song to my fears.

Song by David Kisor: A Love Song to My Fears

I choose to accept my whole self.

I am willing to be present to my fear and let it teach me.

(I am not talking about eminent danger here. I am speaking about those nagging beliefs in the background of our minds that tell us that we, others and life are not enough, we're not ok, we can't…)

A Love Song to My Fears by David Kisor

There will be music and dancing on another night
A celebration to last throughout the years
But tonight I sit and turn out the lights
And sing a love song to my fears

Some night soon there'll be a party with friends and relations
A celebration filled with laughter, jokes and cheers
But tonight I sit in silent contemplation
And sing a love song to my fears

To my deepest disappointment, to every mistake
To the times I turned away, every road I didn't take
To every fault, every flaw, to all that somehow went wrong
I sing to every weakness that somehow makes me strong

Tomorrow may bring a picnic in the park
With sunshine to wipe away these tears
But tonight I sit alone in the dark
And sing a love song to my fears

Oh, oh, oh, oh
To every fault, every flaw, to all that somehow went wrong
I sing to every weakness that somehow makes me strong

Tomorrow I'll be at that pretty picnic in the park
With sunshine to wipe away my tears
But tonight I sit alone in the dark
And sing the song my broken heart needs to hear
It's a love song, a somehow rise above song
A love song to my fears

My First Fear

I was 6 years old. It is nighttime. I am in bed with an older and younger sister. My littlest sibling, almost a toddler, is in a crib nearby. She is crying and dad is yelling and spanking her on her diaper padded seat. Scared breathless, an overwhelming urge washes over me. All I want is to be invisible in order to avoid being hit …in order to be safe.

In my imagination, I appear as a little mummy. Except for my eyes and the tip of my nose, I am entirely wrapped in snowy white strips of crisscrossing cotton cloth. I can see but I am paralyzed to act. I feel sort of safe in this sanitary shell and totally disconnected from life.

For many years I hated that this happened and that things like this happen to any of us. I felt guilty for not helping my sister and scared being noticed.

My human self always wants to feel safe – because it doesn't. And my Spirit knows that safety is. We are evolutionary beings moving through a fear based, past and future based phase of life to a present moment, unconditionally accepting phase of life. When I'm not resisting life – judging it as wrong, there is space and energy for all kinds of things to happen: resourcefulness, responsiveness, resilience, flexibility, creativity…who knows!

Apparently, I wanted to develop the qualities of wisdom, courage, confidence and strength in this lifetime – and moving through my fear of being noticed, was my way of doing that. We can always put a new, more positive perspective/spin on our scary stories – one that empowers us rather than weakens us. Why not? We're making all of our interpretations up anyway.

When I think about billions of galaxies, the precision of the tides, the intricacies of our human bodies, the miraculous migration of butterflies, I have to conclude that there is an orderly intelligence guiding all life - which must include my own. There is a rhyme and reason, something mysterious and absolutely wondrous about life - about my life, just the way it is.

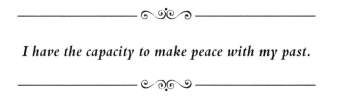

I have the capacity to make peace with my past.

Compassion

I was thinking of a friend the other day. Really, she was more of an acquaintance. We liked each other "ok" but we were so different. I thought she was a bit arrogant. She was ambitious and occasionally she would brag about this or that. Once or twice I thought she had been rude. Even though we got along fine, I never felt a heart connection with her.

A few years ago, she died and I decided to go to the funeral. I was surprised when I walked into the church – it was almost full! I had expected a much smaller gathering. During the service people were invited to share a special memory about their loved one. I was shocked to hear story after story about the kindness and generosity she had expressed. Apparently she had a wonderful sense of humor and she was successful in her line of work. Her success meant success for the company and coworkers and senior management alike, were exceedingly grateful. I thought: I had never seen this person in that light.

Memories of my friend have prompted me to love more generously than facts seem to dictate. She has made it abundantly clear that we are so much more than meets the eye, that we never can see the whole picture about anyone and that maybe it's helpful and even lots more fun to focus on our shared goodness instead of superficial differences.

In this moment, I feel deeply grateful to Rayna for being the messenger through which this truth was revealed to me. Our heart connection is strong and enduring for I am ever thankful for this beautiful insight that brings me such peace and joy.

--- ❧❦❧ ---

*It is never too late to expand our
perspective and compassion.*

*I love because it makes me happy.
I love because...no reason required.*

Love heals and I allow love to express through me.

--- ❧❦❧ ---

Song by Jody and Gary Soland: She Thought He Was Jesus

She Thought He Was Jesus
by Jody and Gary Soland

A little girl, five years old forgotten and alone
Calling the orphanage her home
One day the gardener handed her a rose
And a little child's bible with a note
"Jesus loves you"

And she thought he was Jesus
Through her eyes of innocence
She thought he was Jesus
'Cause Jesus lived in him, Jesus lived in him

Everyday the little girl would anxiously await
The joyful man who met her at the gate
He told her stories and he listened to her fears
And when he left he whispered in her ear
"Jesus loves you"

And she thought he was Jesus
Through her eyes of innocence
She thought he was Jesus
'Cause Jesus lived in him, Jesus lived in him

Time would go by and they both lost touch
She often wondered where he was
She longed to thank the man for helping her
Become who she was
He taught her to love
He taught her to love

A doctor in emergency looked down into the eyes
Of a homeless man fighting for his life
She saw the fear in him and gently took his hand
Just to bring some comfort to the man

Something familiar about his face
Something familiar about his eyes
She couldn't know but it was her turn
To save his life, save his life, save his life

And a homeless man,
Was healed by love that night…

And he though she was Jesus
And his heart knew for sure
He thought she was Jesus
'Cause Jesus lived in her, oh, Jesus lived in her

Oh, the power of love, the power of love
It can heal the world, so
Reach out, won't you reach out
Somebody needs you now… oh, oh, oh

Oh, the power of love, the power of love
Healed that little girl, and she…
Reached out, oh, she reached out
And healed a homeless man…
Oh, the power of love, the power of love
It can heal the world, so
Reach out, reach out, somebody needs you now

Fear Thought

Sometimes I find myself in an old pattern of thinking people don't like me. If people don't like me it means I'm not good enough and that means I'm not safe.

I was sharing this with my friend Jackie and she asked, "When was the first time you remember feeling that way?" I was instantly transported back to 7th grade. At recess, an 8th grade girl was passing out candy and when I asked for some, she said I couldn't have any because she didn't like me. I walked away feeling embarrassed and mad at her and then thinking "something must be wrong with me."

Jackie chimed in, "What if you didn't mind that she said that? How would you feel? What would you think of her?"

In my imagination I was running toward that girl and giving her a big hug! When nothing's wrong – when we don't make that separating judgment – all that's left is love.

During my meditation time later that evening I thought I would try this "not minding" thing out. I didn't have to believe it. I didn't have to take it seriously. I could just be curious and play with the idea of "not minding."

I didn't mind that my mom had died last year. I didn't mind that my best friend had cancer. I didn't mind that George hadn't swept the carpets like he said he would. I didn't mind that I had eaten potato chips and watched a lot of TV. I didn't mind current things that were disturbing. I went back in my life to the things that I had minded a lot, and a little – and I didn't mind them either.

After a while I realized I was experiencing a peacefulness I had only felt a few times in my life. There was a tremendous tenderness in me…an aura of exquisite calm. It was as if I had accidentally wandered into the land of Divine Order. No, it wasn't the order I would have scripted for my life, but it was the order of Life Itself and I felt in perfect harmony with the way it was. In that holy moment, all of the sounds of my life blended into one grand and glorious symphony in the key of perfection!

I am at peace with this moment…as it is.

I cannot change what is
but I can change how I relate to it.
Martha Creek

Living in the Light

Growing up Catholic, I had some confusion about the Sacrament of Confession. My sweet 7 year old self generally created some litany of faults that I thought sounded good to the priest. I wanted to please. When I finally connected that ritual with the shortcomings of my life, I just couldn't confess my sins. I couldn't let Father know I was that bad.

Even though all of this was fabricated in my imagination, it was a real dilemma for me. If I got hit by a car and killed on the way home from school with sin on my heart, I would go to hell forever. I scared myself with that thought for a long time. Even the threat of a fiery, torturous eternity was not enough to make me confess.

I've concluded, there are times when we just can't …whatever. In most instances it's best not to force the issue. I don't have to scare myself into or out of anything. I can be patient with myself and ask for more healing to occur…more wisdom to be exposed. I believe that life is a process and that we can be patient and compassionate with ourselves every step of the way – no matter what!

What eventually happened for me is what I lightheartedly refer to as divine intervention: a new, young priest was assigned to our parish. He seemed to have a more expansive mind and heart and wasn't so concerned with the letter of the law as he was with the spirit of love. Even though this was not common for me, I found the courage within myself to ask him for help.

I believe one of the wisest things we can ever do when facing our problems is to ask for help. It's beneficial to shine a light on our challenging situations because what stays in darkness, expresses as darkness.

Asking for help is an affirmation
that you believe in yourself,
you recognize an answer is available
and you are open to receive it.
Alan Cohen

Our Dark Side

Our dark side is an aspect of ourselves that we've judged as unworthy. It is a part of ourselves that we don't want to associate with. We push that part aside. We hide it and hide from it. We cut ourselves off from those parts of ourselves and then we wonder why we don't feel whole. We instinctively feel that something is missing in our lives.

Recently, I was at a retreat and we were asked to think about divine facets of ourselves. One woman was intrigued by the quality of innocence. That got me thinking about being naïve. I had shoved that value aside because I equated it with not knowing how to do life as I was growing up. I hated that part of myself.

Then we were asked to choose a person in the group that represented that value. The woman I choose was enthusiastic, playful, trusting and open. As I stood in front of her I felt as if I was coming face to face with my naïve self.

I wept with gratitude. I could finally recognize my innocence and beauty. I wept with unbounded joy welcoming my naïve self back into the circle of my love.

The problem wasn't that I was naïve. The problem was that I judged "being naïve" as being less than, not good enough, bad.

For everything there is a season…and we're in it!

What if there really is
-a time to be naïve and a time to express wisdom
-a time to be in darkness and a time to awaken to the light
-a time to be shy and a time to be the life of the party
-a time to be lazy and a time to be industrious
-a time to hold back and a time to give boldly
-a time to be afraid and a time to be perfectly at ease
-a time to stand still and a time to move into new territory
-a time to be addicted and a time to live in freedom
-a time to feel hurt and a time to dance with joy
-a time to eat potato chips and a time to feast on vegetables
-a time to be alone and a time to be with someone
-a time to be invisible and a time to be seen
-a time to be silent and a time to speak up
-a time of deep longing and a time of sweet fulfillment…

Continue making a list of parts of yourself that you have rejected/judged unworthy/don't like, and open to the wonder and beauty of every aspect of your magnificent self.

———————— ༄ ————————

With unconditional love and gratitude
I embrace my whole self
through all of the seasons of my life.

———————— ༄ ————————

Trust

As I was gathering my thoughts to give an inspirational speech, I could feel excitement mounting. It was as if I was cresting the first upper limit curve of a monster roller coaster. I thought, "This is so good! It's really touching my heart! I can hardly wait to share it with everyone tonight!"

As I sat at the computer to put my thoughts on paper, the phone rang. It was my sister. "Could you come over now? I'm feeling kind of funny." I could tell she wasn't in dire distress but I grabbed my car keys. As I was cruising down the expressway I started laughing out loud. I might not be giving that spectacular talk after all. If my sister went in the hospital, even for tests, I would be with her.

My next thought opened up a whole new vista in the landscape of my mind: God's timing is good enough for me. I might never give that talk but that was ok. It was ok if I did and ok if I didn't. I felt complete trust in Life/the Universe/God.

Willingness to rest in trust allows my peace to bubble up to the surface of my life. Living becomes flowing and graceful – unobstructed by expectations and judgments. No strong pushing against, no harsh pulling away from – just a gentle swaying to the heartbeat of the Universe.

Acronym for Trust
Totally Relying Upon Spirit's Timing.

*Life/the Universe/God is taking care of me
more magnificently than I could ever imagine.*

Fear: I wasn't a good enough mom.

I just returned from a family vacation last night. The final 6 hours of riding together in the van were unsettling for me. My granddaughter fussed for a lot of that time. The fussing was annoying but my daughter giving into my granddaughter after she had said no – that was disturbing to me. I think that my daughter is raising a fussy, demanding child.

I didn't teach my daughter enough. I wasn't a good enough mom. I'm mad at myself, irritated with my granddaughter and dismayed and disappointed with my daughter.

How can that be? How can I be so aggravated with those I love so dearly? How can I feel bad about myself for just being the mom that I was? These questions are demanding my attention. OK!

Maybe I could just notice the facts and not put a fearful interpretation on them. How novel! My granddaughter made noise. My daughter gave her an apple. I'm sleepy and would like quiet.

As I dismantled the energetic wall I had constructed with my negative thinking, between my heart and my daughter's, I fell back in love with Elizabeth and myself.

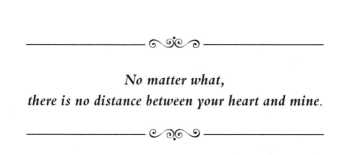

No matter what,
there is no distance between your heart and mine.

Song by David Kisor: No Distance

No Distance by David Kisor

It's been years since I held you in my arms
And rocked you to sleep
Or felt your little hand in mine as we crossed the street.
I always knew you'd spread your wings
Someday you'd go far
But growing up doesn't have to mean we're growing apart

There's no distance between your heart and mine
No distance, no dividing line
No resistance can ever find
Its way between the way we span the tide

A bridge and a bond
No distance, love goes on
Beyond all space and time
No distance, between your heart and mine

I give you love and affection when I know
You're not really mine
We're just kindred Spirits entrusted to each other
For a time
Every lesson taught is a lesson learned
In time every table turns
But as far as I'm concerned this is our eternal sign

There's no distance between your heart and mine
No distance, no dividing line
No resistance can ever find
Its way between the way we span the tide

A bridge and a bond
No distance, love goes on
Beyond all space and time
No distance, between your heart and mine

Any moment, anywhere, hold your hand to your heart
I'm there

No distance between your heart and mine
No distance, do dividing line
No resistance can ever find
Its way between the way we span the tide

A bridge and a bond
No distance, love goes on
Beyond all space and time
No distance, between your heart and mine

It's been years since I held you in my arms
And rocked you to sleep...

Relationships

Sometimes I notice that I can't find happiness and connection because I am looking for love in all the wrong places. I'm looking to my relationships to find something that can only be found inside of me.

I've looked to others for my peace and happiness. I am making them responsible for my state of well being. If people like me, then I feel happy. If it seems they don't care about me, I feel sad. If my daughter or husband do it my way, I feel pleased. If they don't, I sometimes feel mad. I actually feel a little like I'm using them so I can feel better.

After this revelation my thought was, maybe instead of using others, I could just let God/goodness use me. I intuitively felt a peacefulness and joy in that idea. I'm just noticing. I'm noticing how humbling this relationship business can be.

If others don't do things to my satisfaction, I am seeing how manipulative I become in order to get them to change. I often act aloof or I'm very disapproving – and it shows. I can almost feel their hurt. I thought that disapproval was a way to get my way - in order to protect my heart. At the same time I knew that strategy didn't work. No one changed and I felt so separate from the ones I loved the most.

How much time and energy have I used thinking I can't be happy until someone or something changes? How much time and energy have I spent being so mad and sad with myself and others, that I haven't had time and energy to play, to create and to know and live my heart dreams? All of that is changing. I am shifting, thought by thought, into a new way of being.

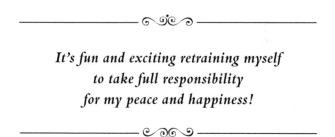

It's fun and exciting retraining myself
to take full responsibility
for my peace and happiness!

Fear: I don't know how to do it right.
I might make things (my life) worse.

I had some congestion and was wondering if I should take herbs, over the counter meds, do nothing or go to the doctor. What's the right thing, the best thing, the most helpful choice? Will any of these options make me breathe easier? What if they (I) make things worse? I was afraid to act.

This little scenario was telling me what I was thinking: I don't know how to do it right – the perfect way. How many times had that thought arisen in my mind?

We can't always do it right, but we can't do it wrong either. Whatever we do, we get feedback to help us make the next decision in present time. In the meantime, we can love each choice, bless each choice, let it be, and wait and see how the process unfolds. And then choose again…or not.

I had identified with (believed) the thought that I didn't know how to do it right. When I think that thought I create that result. I felt weak and confused thinking that thought.

Let's have some fun!

Up until now, I thought that some of my choices could make my life worse. Now, I am willing to trust that every step I take, every decision I make always leads me in the direction of my highest good – no matter what.

*I am always being guided
in the direction of my highest and best!*

Judgment

As a speaker, I find myself critiquing others performances: I like this, I don't like that. Why would they ever say that... and on and on. Pretty soon, I notice what I'm doing – judging the speaker harshly and feeling annoyed with their presentation.

The next time I speak, I observe that I am making similar mistakes in my delivery. It's then that I truly get that I am just like the person I was critical of. Not only am I just like them, but because of our shared human and spiritual identity, I am them! In that moment, compassion washes over me. In my imagination, I am falling down on my knees and asking for and accepting forgiveness for my inconsiderate judgment. This puts me back in love – with myself and them. No guilt, just gratitude and peace for this awareness and experience.

I believe we are one in Spirit. Everyone is connected by the same universal thread of divine love. There is One Presence and we are all a part of it. When I really get that "they" are just a different looking version of "me," I understand that what I do to others, I do to myself. If I give judgment, resentment, anger and blame, I am essentially giving this to myself. If I give love, compassion, forgiveness and kindness, I am essentially giving this to myself.

When I have a decision to make about how I will treat others, I have to ask myself: "How would I like to be treated?" When I know the answer to that question, I know exactly what action to take.

I receive what I give – in that instant!

What Is

I worked too hard and too long yesterday. I prepped my mom's bedroom for painting. I weeded the flower beds around her house again – for the last time. It was my self appointed contribution for many years. As hard as that work was, I am angry at having it taken from me. My sisters and I are preparing to sell our family home.

Sadness washes over me. I want my mom to be alive today. I miss her arm on my arm as we walk into a restaurant every Friday night. I miss being with her every Thursday with my grandkids. I loved that they knew and interacted with their great grandmother. I bragged about this to my friends. I miss her graciously asking me if I could take her to her doctor's appointment. I miss packing up plastic containers of leftovers after weekly Sunday suppers. I can only smile at these cherished memories with longing so deep it hurts.

Ravenous, tired and heavy hearted, I headed home and ate and took a rest. When I got up, George and I went outside to work in our yard. We started out together but 10 minutes into the project, he answered a phone call and then left to take our granddaughters to a festival. I pulled weeds. Several hours later I was exhausted and sat in a heap in front of the TV. I was fuming when George walked in at 10 PM.

For about the last 9 years we have gone through this ritual. I tell George I need help in the yard. I can't and don't want to work like I did for the first 25 years of living on these 18 acres. He seems surprised and acts as if this is the first time he's heard me rant about this.

George should take more responsibility for the yard work! Why do I have to rave like a maniac to get him to understand this? What recourse do I have except to leave? These are the thoughts that are crossing my mind adding incredible fuel to the fire smoldering within me.

I know there is a better way but in my frenzy, I can't seem to admit a new idea or solution and I certainly can't admit any kindness. My angry thoughts are blocking all of that. How would I ever control him? How can I control life and myself without fear and punishment?

Even in my frustration I know that all of this is a bit silly. I know that George is not who is the matter with me. I know that I can't control life – even though I want to with all my might. I want my mom to be alive. I want to be able to physically do what was possible for me when I was younger and stronger. I want George to do something he has no interest in. He doesn't see the yard as a mess. He doesn't have my need for orderliness to feel comfortable.

I understand that I am the one who is resisting what is and that's what's the matter. It feels so painful wanting life to be different than it is. I comprehend that clearly in the words I have just written. As I pause and breathe deeply, I catch myself opening to the natural flow of ever changing life. A window of grace has opened and I am starting to feel a sense of calm approaching.

Fear: I could hurt someone.

I am just beginning to feel a sense of calm approaching. Even though my heart is not smiling this very minute I will apologize to the man I love so dearly. I told George I would figure out how to get the yard work done. He was visibly grateful. Then he said our daughter was coming tomorrow to mulch the trees. The storm was over. That storm was over.

George said he had been thinking about helping out more. He wanted to know what he could do right then and there and he worked hard outside for an hour or so. When he came in feeling sick, I began to worry that pushing him to work in the yard might cause him to have a heart attack.

That was my greatest fear – that I could hurt someone, even inadvertently. This expanded into the fear that I could hurt someone so badly they would commit suicide. It's why I was cautious about life, about stepping out in the world more fully and saying what I wanted or how I felt. It's why I held back in a thousand ways.

I have been wrestling with this fear for many years. It just slipped into my awareness somewhere along the line.

I have never contemplated committing suicide but now I think that thought was about me…that I could hurt so much, I wouldn't want to live. I think that was why I was so desperate to control life and why I got so scared when I couldn't control others. It's why I considered stepping out of the chaos of life and planting melons and tomatoes – staying firmly rooted in my fenced in garden.

But through the years, I have had a change of heart…a tremendous shift in perspective. I hope you can catch a glimpse of my metamorphosis in the stories I am sharing.

I have learned so much about peace filled living. It makes me eager to open completely to life in all its majesty and mystery. There is a YES that's alive in me that I'm just beginning to become acquainted with. That's what I want to explore, experience and express! That's why I have decided to sing my heart song in these pages.

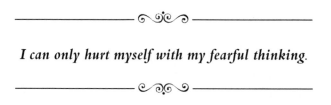

I can only hurt myself with my fearful thinking.

Song by Jody and Gary Soland: Becoming Who You Are

Becoming Who You Are by Jody and Gary Soland

Copyright 2012

Just today, I heard you say
You wished you knew
Who it is, you really are
And what you're here to do

I believe
You're a shining star
And how I love watching you
Becoming who you are

You've walked around, upon the ground
You've learned how to survive
But something deep, inside your soul
Is reaching for the sky

I believe
You're a shining star
And how I love, watching you
Becoming who you are

Oh, it's just a matter of time
Before you're gonna shine…

You're changing things, you're growing wings
You're learning how to fly
You're letting go, and now you know
All the reasons why

I believe
You're a shining star
And how I love, watching you
Becoming who you are.

Oh, how I love watching you
Becoming who you are

Looking Through the Eyes of Love

In order to view myself in a more expansive way – beyond old, limiting, fearful beliefs of who I thought I was - it has been helpful to state: "I am the one/woman/man" – instead of using my name. This proved an easy, comfortable way to begin to see my self in a new light.

I am the one/woman/man/ who lives her/his dreams.
I am the one who allows herself to be happy.
I am the one who welcomes happiness with open arms.
I am the one who walks in confidence, love and wisdom.
I am the one who lives in her idea of integrity - no matter what.
I am the one who delights in life.
I am the one who laughs wholeheartedly.
I am the one who keeps her focus on her wondrous dreams.
I am the one who expresses great insight and clarity.
I am the one who respects and honors her inner knowing.
I am the one who tells the truth in kind ways.
I am the one who confidently moves into greater joy.
I am the one who puts down the dead weight of past, painful thinking.
I am the one who is naturally present in love.
I am the one who relaxes into life.
I am the one who is loving what is. Yahoo!
I am the one who is confident and joyful being seen and heard.
I am the one who loves herself – no matter what!
I am the one who is willing to feel great all of the time.
I am the one who trusts that life is working on her behalf.
I am the one who is financially successful.
I am the woman who allows love to flow through her and to her…

How would you like to see yourself?
Are you willing to put some ideas on this page?

We don't have to go digging up our past to find out what is causing our present upset. We only have to be aware of what is happening in the "now moment" and we will discover the thoughts that are causing us pain.

Fear: If I don't feel "better than" someone, I'm not safe.

I went to the dinner theatre with family and friends. I brought plain food with me because of sinus and chest congestion. My friend Tina didn't need special food. She conversed with my mom in a light hearted and caring way. My contribution to the conversation seemed abrupt and flat. I found myself feeling small and depressed as we walked toward our front row seats. The first act began and instantly I felt overwhelmed. I endured the performance.

Alone with George in the car on the way home, my anger exploded! Luckily for me, he stayed neutral as I lashed out and felt my feelings.

In a few minutes, I settled down and had the realization that this upset was about me when I think someone is better than me. Then, I feel like I'm not safe. Pretty scary thought! I believed/identified with – the thought that if I didn't feel better than someone, I wasn't safe. That concept can throw a real wrench into any relationship!

True humility means letting go of identification with thoughts that tell us we're "better than" and thoughts that tell us we're "less than." True humility is experiencing oneness with all creation. It expresses as a willingness to flow with the highs and lows of our lives without making too much of either…or celebrating it all! It expresses as respectfulness and reverence for the innate value of all life.

I know that I am one with all that is.

Gratitude

As a child, I was taught to say thank you for gifts. It was good manners – but my focus was on the gift, not the gratitude. It took something very big and very special for me to feel sincerely grateful.

Then gratitude expanded to include everyday things I often took for granted and I find myself awakening with thoughts like: I'm so grateful I can see, or have running water in my house or garbage service.

A favorite quote from Alan Cohen says: "Learn to say thank you for everything and you will find that everything is a gift." Now my practice includes being grateful for all of it – even though at the time, I don't feel appreciative for such things as interruptions or disagreements. I am grateful anyway. Sometimes I'm rewarded with knowing what the blessing is. Often, I never know – but the sweet peace I experience trusting that life is working on my behalf - in all circumstances - is gift enough.

Last week I felt rejection and for a fleeting moment a wave of sadness cascaded over me and the next moment I laughed out loud and felt totally and excitedly grateful because I knew I was being redirected – to write this book.

Focusing on being shut out… hell.
Focusing on what is opening up to me…heaven.

My gratitude generates an attitude
of abundance and joy.

Gratitude is my greatest ally in living joyfully.

Song by Karen Drucker: I'm So Grateful

I'm So Grateful

Words and music: Karen Drucker
from Songs of the Spirit 4
Copyright: TayToones Music, BMI

Gratitude before me
Gratitude behind me
Gratitude to the left of me
Gratitude to the right of me
Gratitude above me
Gratitude below me
Gratitude within me
Gratitude around me

I'm so grateful
I'm so grateful
I'm so grateful
I'm so grateful

Gratitude before me
Gratitude behind me
Gratitude to the left of me
Gratitude to the right of me
Gratitude above me
Gratitude below me
Gratitude within me
Gratitude around me

I'm so grateful
I'm so grateful
I'm so grateful
I'm so grateful

Gratitude before me
Gratitude behind me
Gratitude to the left of me
Gratitude to the right of me
Gratitude above me
Gratitude below me
Gratitude within me
Gratitude around me

I'm so grateful
I'm so grateful
I'm so grateful
I'm so grateful

Purpose

I started a Montessori preschool with a dear friend. In a way, this just fell into my life. My girlfriend's son was around three years old and she wanted a preschool for him to attend in her neighborhood – so I said yes, I would do that. I sometimes doubted that this was my purpose because it didn't come directly from me. Then a musician friend shared something that made me think about this differently. He said, when something came toward him, he stepped toward it. And that is what I had done. I was living on purpose – I was just unaware of it at the time!

I believe, with all my heart, that we are all living on purpose. But sometimes when I think about the great accomplishments of others, I still can feel small and lazy and I think I'm not living intentionally.

I found myself writing about this in my journal. What came to mind was that we can never fully know whose life we will touch with our words and actions. We never know who that person's life will touch and whose life theirs will touch in ever widening ripples of interconnection and love.

It could be a book by a great scientist that makes a positive difference in someone's life, but it could also be a smile or a hug or a kind word that does the very same thing.

I know this: we are all equally important and each of us has an essential part to play in this life. We are all living on purpose.

My purpose is to love.

Defining Moment

When I was 15, I thought I was so neat. I had a best girl friend. High school was fun. I felt pretty and smart I was asked to the prom – an exciting prospect. I had to beg mom and dad to let me go. Even though my older sister hadn't started dating and I was young, my parents reluctantly said yes. Preparations advanced. My cousin's fancy dress was altered. I made an appointment with the hairdresser.

I went to the dance but that's all I recall. A few days later, mom asked me if I had gone to confession. Very nonchalantly I said that it wasn't any of her business. Where that response came from is a mystery to this day. I hardly talked to mom. I never gave back talk. "March up to your room young lady." I was mortified. Dad came up like a raging volcano and all of his fiery anger and fear erupted across my face. I was stunned. I was ashamed. How could this be happening? How could I have said something so stupid?

Just as I was beginning to blossom, just as it was about time for me to be attaining independence from my parents, one small step at a time, I contracted in fear.

The fear lay buried in the background of my life, rising when I would attempt to be out in the world more fully. I would enthusiastically step on the gas and then shortly afterwards abruptly stomp on the brakes.

I wanted to be safe, and I also wanted to soar! But how could I with the fearful thoughts: I can't trust myself. I might do it wrong. I might do something bad. I'm bad. Impossible!

I clearly remember making the decision not to let my dad ever see my heart again. I kept that promise...for awhile. That episode ended and life went on. I limped forward. Time healed some of the riff. Wisdom and love has healed all of the rest.

My dad was a gentle, shy man who cared deeply about our family. But in this instance, his fear seemed to overtake him. I've been there myself. And when this happens, we can say and do things that are so unlike love; that can be so hurtful and unkind.

And yet this wound eventually opened me to greater compassion for all of us under the controlling influence of our fearful thinking. It crystallized my desire to find skillful, more considerate ways to work through differences. I became more willing to open to greater wisdom and understanding which could shepherd me back to love.

It takes spiritual vision to see past appearances to our natural innocence. It takes an incredible shift in perspective to open to and live from a consciousness of love rather than fear. I'm learning! I'm practicing! I'm living in love more and more! I love you dad.

The more I choose to stay "in love," the easier life is.

Forgiveness

I was feeling hurt and mad about something and I just wanted to cry my pain and feel compassion for myself…and I did. I allowed myself to be where I was, without hurting anyone with my strong feelings or making myself wrong. I wanted to let go of this upset but I didn't want to force superficial forgiveness. I also didn't want to make anyone wrong. The moment I do that, I make myself a victim. I am crystal clear that I don't want to live life as a victim. In my heart of hearts, I know I do not want to be a revengeful person either. That's not me. I'd rather put my attention, my energy on living my dreams. But my anger toward others and thinking that I'm being left out in the cold continued to recycle over and over in my mind. Even as I cry about this, I freely say "thank you" and think maybe what feels like an ending is opening me up to a new beginning. There's a little place in me that says "yes" to the possibility that this experience is unfolding for my highest and best. Even the fact that I think this experience might possibly be unfolding – is a miracle. Often, I just feel stuck.

Tonight I don't feel so good about myself and my accomplishments, about how I am being treated and life in general. I ask a higher power to help me through this then I cry myself to sleep.

I woke up the next morning thinking about the bible story of Joseph and his coat of many colors. Joseph's brothers were jealous of him and so they stole his colorful coat and left him to die. In the end, they decided to sell him into slavery to make money. In captivity, someone lied about him and ruined his reputation. These are some of the worst things that can befall any of us and yet, Joseph wasn't distracted by these things. He just kept doing what was his to do and eventually he became the overseer of the Pharaoh's grain. When Joseph's brothers came asking for food, they recognized him and begged for forgiveness. Joseph replied, "Do not be afraid, even though you meant what happened for evil, God meant it for good."

I wondered how I could reinterpret what was happening in my life, from the vantage point of "this is meant for my good." I knew if I didn't, I was going to be pretty miserable. Thinking that I'm being shut out, mistreated, that I'm not good enough is painful with a capital P.

Forgiveness is not about staying in an abusive situation or even being friends with the person we're forgiving. It is about giving up the struggle of wanting life to be different than it is. It is about trusting that life is working on our behalf – even when we can't see that. It is about moving away from what is painful and toward what is life giving and love filled. Forgiveness is having the courage to free our hearts to love again. We do it for our own sake, for our own peace and happiness.

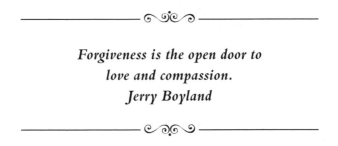

Forgiveness is the open door to
love and compassion.
Jerry Boyland

I am ready to walk through that door.

Off Track Again!

I was feeling centered, peaceful and confident. I was experiencing happiness. It felt heavenly…and then boom! In an instant, I find I'm really angry at myself or something or someone. I'm beginning to feel as if I am at the beginning again – right back where I started before my vision went blank. The eye operations, feeling my feelings, being with what is, the fears appearing, the exploration of those fears, the connecting to a sense of purpose – what has it all been for?

I just feel mad today and I don't want to get over it. I don't want to do anything to feel better. I just don't care. And so I eat and watch lots of TV and feel confused. I am mad at myself and I'm projecting that on to others. I must be doing something wrong. I compassionately smile at that old, familiar thought pattern. (That's something that would not have happened at the beginning of this journey.)

But how can I keep doing everything "right" physically, mentally, emotionally, and spiritually to get the results I want? Something in me says, "You can't Nanc, **and** you don't have to. Could you allow a tiny ray of light in? Is there any room in your heart to love what is? Do you know for sure that you've messed up, slid backwards? Is it possible you could be grateful for the way it is for you today? When you don't make "what is" – all wrong, things have room to shift all by themselves."

It's pretty exhausting thinking I need to control every aspect of my life to feel safe and happy. I am coming to the realization that life is not about controlling it at all. It is about thinking thoughts that align with peace instead of pain. It's about loving the way it is and always loving myself. As I do this, I allow life, in all of its beauty and wonder, to live through me. That seems a lot easier and more relaxing than trying to make life conform to my expectations.

I think I had taken a pretty big stride into greater joy and I have been bringing myself back to an old, familiar way of feeling by being upset and eating and moping. I choose to believe that I am getting used to a greater capacity/experience of centeredness, peacefulness and confidence one graceful step forward and a step or 2 backwards at this time. This is another opportunity to strengthen my "come back to center" muscle and I am grateful.

It feels as if the Universe is tenderly rocking me back and forth between the worlds of fear and faith until I can move forward and stand steady and sure in my new found love for myself and life. I will be gentle and patient with myself as I remember that all of the learning and practice I've done has not been in vain. I truly am capable of returning to center more easily and quickly than ever before. I really am spending more time being "in love."

———————— ⬥ ————————

I allow my life to unfold in ease and grace,
in gentleness and joy.

———————— ⬥ ————————

Smiling

There was a time when I was afraid to travel alone because I thought I wouldn't be able to take care of myself. I got frightened at a weekend workshop and scary thoughts began to filter through my mind whenever I contemplated going somewhere without family or friends.

Intermittently I continued to travel solo with varying results. Once in awhile I would experience comfort but more often than not, I would feel terrified. To some extent, it was helpful to select more positive thoughts when anxious ideas appeared out of the blue.

But what proved even more effective was the practice of smiling compassionately at my uneasy thoughts. Sometimes I even find myself laughing out loud at them! Occasionally I will pat myself gently on the shoulder and say: "It's ok honey. I love you."

When I do this, I don't automatically believe all of my thoughts. I'm not pulled so blindly into drama. I don't create solid proof about my righteousness and I don't scare myself with them. I just don't get scared and feel uncomfortable with my thoughts. I smile at them kindheartedly and like colorful hot air balloons they lightly float across the sky of my mind until they are out of sight.

―――――――――― ⌒ ᓀᓂᓀ ⌒ ――――――――――

I pay no attention to the negativity of my mind.

―――――――――― ⌒ ᓀᓂᓀ ⌒ ――――――――――

Early in the spring, I had the yearning to go on a retreat away from home by myself. There was no anxiety about this – just a clear knowing; an automatic trust that I would be just fine. I also knew that if scary thoughts did arise, I would cradle them in my love.

I had the most relaxing trip of my life!

Healing

Last night, I did some healing work. Little Nancy, in the open jail cell in my heart, held my hand and together we walked beyond the prison bars. The image of that mummy figure of myself when dad spanked my sister, came to me to remove her bandages. A picture of myself sitting on a green chair after dad hit me for saying it was none of mom's business if I had gone to confession, appeared. She was gagged with a big white rag, had disheveled short hair and she wore a multicolored jacket that looked messy and old. She looked crazed – for trying to control so much over the years to feel safe. She asked me to hold her hand. She said she wanted to be healed. In my imagination I untied the gag.

Now I continue to feel as if I am going to die – choke to death with this whooping cough. I know all of this could be symbolic of me dying to an old way of being and seeing and I make the decision to allow the belief that I am/was bad – to die.

The coughing when I lay down is noticeably better. I still feel like I am hardly sleeping. This concerns me and yet I keep reminding myself of the truth: everything is good and all is well.

I make peace with my past.

As I lay down the dead weight
of past, painful thinking
I restore my joy in living.

Letting Go Again

Straightening out my "school closet" and thinking about letting go of all of the books, activities and lesson plans – even though I don't use them – just feels too hard. Each page and paper has been such a sweet companion through most of my life. It feels like letting go of them is letting go of a part of my heart.

The fears I am thinking about laying down feel like such sweet companions too – that I've used to help me feel safe through the years

And yet, there is a willingness to release my fears because I have adopted and integrated new beliefs into my life. I feel absolutely safe and my heart is peaceful. I have given myself more breathing room. I am more curious and excited about coming alive to myself and to life.

And so with great confidence, peace, gratitude and joy, I release the thought form and the energy of the belief that I could hurt someone so much they would commit suicide.

In the past, I believed I could hurt someone so much they would commit suicide. Now I am willing to see and believe that in obvious and unexplained ways I am a blessing and benefit to everyone – we all are…no matter what.

I am a gift.

Song by Karen Drucker and Karen Taylor-Good: I Am a Gift

I Am a Gift

Words and Music by Karen Drucker and Karen Taylor-Good
from The Call
Copyright: TayToones Music, BMI

I am a gift
No matter what age
No matter how I look
There's beauty in each stage

I am a gift
And I promise everyday
When I look in the mirror I'll say
I am a gift

I am a gift
I've loved really well
And every year I've lived
Has a different tale to tell

I've made mistakes
Have some regrets
But I promise I'll never forget
I am a gift…I am a gift

There may be times when I forget the truth about me
When it seems time and youth are just marching on without me
That's when I might need you to find me
And ever so gently remind me

That I am a gift...a precious child
I'm put here on this earth but only for awhile

So I make this vow and I say it with love
I am perfect and whole and enough

I am a gift...I am a gift

There may be times when I forget the truth about me
When it seem time and youth are just marching on without me
That's when I might need you to find me
And ever so gently remind me

That I am a gift...a precious child
I'm put here on this earth but only for awhile
I make this vow and say it with love
I am perfect and whole and enough

I am a gift...I am a gift...I am a gift...

Truth

I have hives! This felt like part of the "free fall" into old, familiar, not so good feelings after feeling especially centered. The itch and pain seemed unbearable at times. Not only was I feeling miserable physically, I was emotionally distraught as well. When I feel physical distress, it's not always easy for me to stay calm and peaceful. I was angry and afraid. This fury spilled over to others. But when I thought about it, I was really mad at myself. I had been criticized for asking a question and I went into an old pattern of "how stupid of me." I recalled several other examples of me thinking I was bad. If I'm bad, there must be a need for punishment. Guilty feelings often express as pain. This was a recycling of once adopted patterns.

I had a huge, pitiful cry. I was avoiding this for awhile because I thought it could make me stuffy on top of the itch – doubling my misery. It did. Now I couldn't breathe from my nose. It actually felt swollen completely shut.

In the height of my frenzy (thank goodness) I remembered something I had read earlier in the day. It was a quote by Peace Pilgrim: "If you realized how powerful your thoughts are, you would never think a negative thought." I also remembered Emmet Fox saying: "release all problems to a higher power."

Here was an opening; movement away from my negative, pessimistic, depressing thoughts that could never bring me peace. I began taking easy, full breaths – from my mouth, which helped me relax and become less fearful. I gave myself encouraging suggestions: I am willing to feel good.

I turn my problem over to a higher power. I trust that life is working on my behalf. I entreated my stuffed up nose to remember its purpose for being. I affirmed: I breathe freely and easily. I apologized to myself for thinking I was bad. In that moment, I refused to see myself as less than a perfect expression and experience of unconditional love. That's my true nature. That's the truth at the heart of it all for me.

In my imagination, I could hear these thoughts: "You can pretend you are "bad" all you want. I'm not buying it. You know the truth of who you are. You just forgot for a moment."

Within 20 minutes, I could breathe easily. The fire on my skin had completely faded. I apologized to George for my angry outburst. I could see where I had veered into troubled waters with thinking I was bad. I experienced the results of changing my mind about that. Once again, I was deeply rooted in truth, and I felt perfectly peaceful and happy. The next morning, my hives were gone - for good.

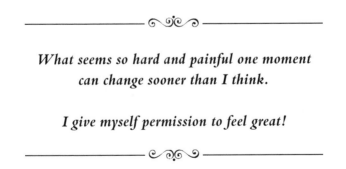

What seems so hard and painful one moment can change sooner than I think.

I give myself permission to feel great!

Song by Karen Drucker and John Hoy: Healed Whole and Healthy

Healed, Whole and Healthy

Words: Karen Drucker; Music: Karen Drucker and John Hoy
from Songs of the Spirit 2
Copyright: TayToones Music, BMI

Healed, Whole, Well…

I am healed, whole and healthy
I relax and visualize
I am healed, whole and healthy
I am well – I am well.

I am healed, whole and healthy
I relax and visualize
I am healed, whole and healthy
I am well – I am well.

I am healed, whole and healthy
I accept and I receive
I am healed, whole and healthy
I am well – I am well.

I am healed, whole and healthy
Angels are watching over me
I am healed, whole and healthy
I am well – I am well.

I am healed, whole and healthy
I've got love surrounding me
I am healed, whole and healthy
I am well – I am well.

I am healed, whole and healthy
I've got love surrounding me
I am healed, whole and healthy
I am well – I am well.
All is well – I am well.

Life

I was greeted by a million precious moments this past week:

A niece's husband died suddenly and unexpectedly:
–family coming together to offer loving support,
–hundreds of visitors at the funeral home,
–heart warming and humorous memories shared,
–neighbors bearing casseroles, cleaning house, caring for the new puppy.
–the funeral procession passing the court house – sidewalks lined with police officers, judges and acquaintances standing shoulder to shoulder in tribute to their friend.

Another niece got married. The wedding took place without her dad who had died a year and a half earlier:
–her mom and brother walking her down the isle,
–a picture of her dad thoughtfully tucked into her bouquet,
–grandma's dazzling broach decorating the wedding cake,
–her brother reaching out and tenderly touching the strings our hearts with harmonizing chords of welcome and celebration. Their dad would have been bursting with pride.

On Sunday afternoon I went to my uncle's 90th birthday party. Sharing a meal and watching a slide show of the family's shining moments through the years, I cried more genuinely and laughed more wholeheartedly than I have in a long, long time.

In the midst of all of this, I remembered what my friend Larry Watson had written in his book *Rough Pieces*: "This world is just as precious as the next one. We can find our heaven here." That idea expanded in me: This second is just as precious as the next one. We can find our happiness here.

A passing remembrance of times I had wished something to be finished before it began washed over me. I felt the momentary sensation of being bored, of not knowing what to do or say, of wanting things to be different than they were.

And then almost instantaneously something shifted and I was present. I received each moment with an open mind and heart. I graciously played with every opportunity as it presented itself. There was a river of great joy and great sorrow flowing through my heart. Moment by moment, my life was full of the sheer mystery and wonder of living and dying.

Heaven is the joyful experience of allowing love to flow to us and through us.

We don't have to die to live in heaven! Susan Douthitt

I went to a wedding several weeks later. It didn't feel like I was receiving each moment with an open mind and heart or graciously playing with every opportunity. In fact, I found myself sitting alone at a table in the reception hall. The amazing thing is that I didn't make that/me wrong.

Perhaps I was meeting the moment with an open heart after all – because I felt perfectly peaceful. I smiled in sheer gratitude for being "at peace/in peace" with the way it was.

Song by David Kisor: Miriam

Miriam by David Kisor

Miriam is a little girl
Sensitive and kind
Her special gift is the way she lives
She thinks with her heart and feels with her mind

Miriam is a wonderful friend
Helps through the hurt and the healing
Through good and bad she always has
The power to feel the feeling

When someone cries, she cries
When someone laughs, she laughs
She kicks every stone, smells every flower
All along life's path

She says, "Live each moment as it passes by
This moment is all we have."
Miriam knows how to cry, she knows how to laugh

Miriam grows and meets a boy
Sensitive and kind
His special gift is the way he lives
He thinks with his heart and feels with his mind.

Miriam loves being a wife and mother
She works through the hurt and the healing
As the family grows, everyone knows
The power to feel the feeling

When someone cries, she cries
When someone laughs, she laughs
They kick every stone, smell every flower
All along life's path

They say, "Live each moment as it passes by
This moment is all we have."
Miriam knows how to cry, she knows how to laugh

Miriam sits in a wheelchair
Takes a long nap everyday
When she lifts her grey hair, I'm there
To hear what she has to say

Miriam talks 'bout her family and friends
Remembers the hurt and the healing
Through her life's history, she gives to me
The power to feel the feeling

And when she cries, I cry
When she laughs, I laugh
I'll kick every stone, smell every flower
All along life's path

I'm going to live each moment as it passes by
This moment is all we have
Miriam taught me to cry
With the wonder of life in her eyes
Miriam knows how to cry, she knows how to laugh

Another Point of View

This morning an enormous swing set was delivered to our house. George found a bargain. Two workers were here to assemble it. I didn't even say good morning to the men. I didn't want that "large bargain" placed in my beautifully landscaped yard. Besides, the grand kids are just about too old to play on it.

I barked to the workers where it "couldn't" go and went back into the house. Still, there was a bit of confusion about the placement. It ended up in a position that was unacceptable to me. George noted that I should have been outside for the entire time to get this straight. I started to defend myself but instead I opened to another possibility: maybe George was right. If I wanted it a certain way, it could have been helpful to have been there to see it done to my satisfaction. I was grateful that the handy men went to the extra trouble of turning the swing set when I asked to have it repositioned.

Reflecting on this incident later, I was stunned and embarrassed that I had been so short with the workers and George. It was impossible not to notice my inflexibility and my subtle resentment at not getting my way. In addition, I was mad at myself for acting mean. Negativity multiplied!

When George came in, he was laughing at Ria's antics and sharing how this funny dog had been slinking around on the plastic slide laying in the grass. I became aware that I was prompting myself; "it's ok to laugh, let yourself be happy Nanc." George and I giggled together about how silly that dog had been.

My resentment about getting a swing set, my negative self talk - I chose to let that go. I realized this was working out for all of us. George was getting the play set he wanted for our granddaughters and it was placed in a way that was pleasing to me.

Lately, I'm noticing that I am being a great coach and cheerleader to myself. I am supporting myself with loving thoughts and choices that really do promote inner peace and joy. I find I am encouraging myself to be happy, to be a part of, to release negative thinking and replace it with something more optimistic. I am teaching myself how to be happy and I have been willing to follow my instructions.

When I sense that upset feeling starting to arise in me – that's the time I find I am remembering to pause and shift back into the reality of love. This has been a surprisingly satisfying experience that gets easier each time I do it.

I inspire and encourage myself to live from joy.

Love is Always There

In the early 90's a book came out entitled *Magic Eye: A New Way of Looking at the World* by N. E. Thing Enterprises. On each page of the book there was a colorful pattern. That was it. However, by gazing at the abstract pattern for a few minutes, a three dimensional image would appear – seemingly out of nowhere. The entire page could look like repeated squiggles of blue and pink but by gazing at it in a certain way, a 3 dimensional object would pop out in clear view.

That concept/book reminded me that love is present all of the time. We just don't always see it at first glance. Our opinions judgments, need to be right, our anger, resentments, regrets, feeling bad about ourselves, negative self talk, making others wrong – all stemming from fearful thinking, are like clouds that cover love up – that hide it from view. The love is there but it's impossible to see it from a negative perspective.

It takes a different way of viewing life, a different way of viewing the habitual, everyday patterns of our lives, in order to see the underlying pattern of all creation – unconditional love. When we see life through the eyes of love, love is all that we can experience.

Inner and Outer Vision

My eyes are strong and healthy.
I see the beauty and goodness life has to offer.
I view myself and others with
compassion and good will.
I envision a world of peace and harmony and
I honor and appreciate my
precious sight and insight.

Blessing upon blessing to all those
who support us in seeing clearly.

Inner Freedom

It is my hope that I have offered simple yet powerful ways we can perceive life through a new lens. I encourage us to play with some of these practices and see if they have positive value and meaning. I hope they support, empower and inspire all of us to live from a consciousness of love…to live the love that we are.

These practices and perspectives are like wings that gracefully uphold me as I soar to the melodies of my heart; as I tune into and confidently live my most cherished dreams. They continue to open my heart and mind to new, life filled possibilities and to the perfection of the moment. They support me in choosing to experience life from the vantage point of love in whatever situation I am in, or whatever emotion I am experiencing. They remind me of the truth that I am whole and complete and enough – no matter what.

*I have finally found my wings
and I am unafraid to use them.*

Song by Jody and Gary Soland: Wings

Wings by Jody and Gary Soland

I had built a wall around my heart
Brick by brick I worked all day 'till dark
Till I made a fortress for my fear
A wall of strong resistance standing here

Then Spirit whispered softly to my heart
Do you want to stay right where you are
I could free you if you'd only trust
We'll break through those walls, the two of us

Or maybe you will use your wings
And you will fly right over
And then you'll see, that you are free
To follow me with the wings I gave you

Suddenly, my fear was fading fast
I felt Spirit's wings upon my back
Funny how the walls came tumbling down
About the time I let go of the ground

For I have finally found my wings
And I can fly right over
And now I see,
That I am free
To fly
With the wings that Spirit gave me…

Wings…
To fly…
To soar through
My sky
No fear
No doubt
I'm free to fly right now

I had built a wall and now it's gone
I can trust that Spirit leads me on
Nothing's gonna hold me back again
I'm letting go and sailing on the wind

Oh, I have learned to use my wings
And I can fly right over
And now I see
That I am free
To fly
With wings…wings
My wings…my wings…my wings

A New Beginning

I went out to garden this crisp, clear autumn day. Well, it's not officially autumn but the kids are back in school and the early morning mist, as it silently dances off the lake, insinuates the shift that is taking place in the seasons of life.

I am grateful for the many shifts that have taken place in me, through many seasons. I am less fearful and more trusting in life as it is. I am more accepting of who I am, right where I am. I am more generous in my thoughts about myself and others; less judgmental. I clearly see that life is the eternal process of being: being the seed and the growth and the flower and the fruit to become the seed again; silent, still and filled with promise.

We hold the seeds of our fulfillment in our hearts. May we plant and nourish those seeds that bring joy and peace to our lives. And then may we touch the lives of others with our joy and peace until the whole world has become its own promise, its own sweet fulfillment, its own experience of peace and joy.

My garden vacillates between sharing colorful swatches of vivacious golden marigolds and the dusty, rusty browns of dehydrated tomato bushes – signaling of the end of a season. It's time to put my garden to bed and time to put my pen to rest.

I echo the words of my cherished friend and teacher Pat Barker when I say: because every ending contains the seed of a new beginning, the last page of this little book is not the end of our journey, but a continuing, a deepening and an awakening to the incredible and immeasurable power of love.

I love you! I love me! I love life! Peace, Nancy

*I allow the light of love that I
am to shine brilliantly
through the eternal seasons of my life.*

Karen Drucker has recorded 15 CDs of her original inspirational music, and is the author of an inspirational book, "Let Go of the Shore: Stories and Songs That Set the Spirit Free." In following her passion, Karen sings, speaks, leads women's retreats and has been called "a master of communicating presence and spirituality through music." She loves making music, making a difference, and touching hearts. You can find out more about Karen and her work at www.karendrucker.com

David Kisor is a songwriter, teacher, and performer who lives and works in Cincinnati, Ohio. As Music Director at the New Thought Unity Center he has written for solo voice, choir and congregation. His songs written and recorded for *Growing Sound* promote positive social-emotional development in young children. He has also written extensively for family and children's musical theater. His life's work is filling the world with love and laughter through the gift of words and music.

Jody Soland's passion and purpose is quickly evident to anyone who has the pleasure of experiencing the gifts she brings. Jody has the ability to connect with her audiences, brings exceptional vocals, and has unique skill for capturing and delivering a message that deeply moves people, heart and soul. Open, engaging, kind, compassionate, inspiring, heartfelt, passionate, witty, thought provoking and empowering. To find out more about Jody and her work you can contact her at <u>www.jodysoland.com</u>